Color Vision

By:

Tyrelle H.C.

Edited with Akeem Shannon

Copyright ManMan Publishing, LLC © 2021

Table of Contents

4. Color Vision
6. Map
8. Black is Beauty
10. Attention
12. Parasite
14. Passion dreams
16. Mule
18. Deserts
20. Ghost
22. Gambling
24. Actor
26. True Colors
28. Shatter
30. Periodt
32. The Mask
34. Replacement
36. Northern lights
38. Comet
40. Promise
42. Nurse
44. You, Always
46. Teddy Bear
48. Brain builder
50. Judgment
52. Cybernetic sadness
54. Writer God
56. Panic Attack
58. Just Keep Swimming
60. Drop of Lies
64. Colorful Ending

Foreword

On February 7, 2018, a young man met a young entrepreneur. The meeting was scheduled by Big Brothers Big Sisters of Eastern Missouri and the goal was to make a "match" – to pair a man with a boy, with the consent of his mother, to see each other, in-person, for a minimum of four hours a month. The Little Brother Tyrelle Henley Jr. is the author of ColorVision and his Big Brother, Akeem Shannon, is a natural-born leader and mentor.

For over a century, the expectation of a Big Brother has been to serve as a role model and guide to a "Little," sometimes cheering him on and other times interrupting and redirecting.

In a world that frequently gravitates to immediate solutions and names winners and losers, it's no surprise that identifying the challenges in a young person's life and helping him overcome these hardships are prioritized.

And while this approach can be appropriate and even essential, Big Brother Akeem forged a different conversation. He looked to Tyrelle's strengths, believing in his Little's existing interests, thoughts, and dreams as the true building blocks of positive growth.

This book is a testament to their relationship. To the idea that everyone, irrespective of life's challenges or uncertainties, has inherent strengths, skills, and passions; and that our world should be seen in its full, natural abundance – filled with endless opportunities to do better and more.

Tyrelle and Akeem teach us to stop looking for the struggles and complications and begin affirming the good that already exists. This paradigm shift can reposition a Big Brother as a partner, helping unleash within his Little Brother a new spirit - sparking new ideas and thoughts, challenging his imagination and giving life to his dreams. This book, so beautifully written and designed by Tyrelle, is a result of this transformational approach.

Everyone is blazing their own path. Tyrelle's marking his path through poems, evidence of a personal passage carved, dreams realized, and a legacy that will endure.

Rebecca J. Hatter
President/CEO
Big Brothers Big sisters of Eastern Missouri

Hello my name is Tyrelle, I'm 15 years old, and I like to talk to people about what's on their mind. Color Vision is a book about my life and brings you into my dream world. This book is a collection of 30 stories that I can't wait for you to read. The stories are for teens and adults, who can't always explain their emotions. Each of these stories will help you understand my point of view.
Get ready to travel into Color Vision!

- Tyrelle H.C.

Color Vision

Red as magma.
Red as fire.
Blue as a cold wave or your salty tears.
Yellow as light bulbs, but bright as the sun.
Green as slime, frogs, or Oscar the Grouch.

Black as a shadow in darkness.
Black as the coat of a Panther.
White as a blank page or walls that surround me.
Pink as cherry blossoms, but lustrous as a diamond.
Purple as nymphaea, starlings or amethyst.

There's a rainbow living inside of you.
This is color vision at its finest.
It's the hardest thing to see, but important to study.
So embrace your feelings, because these colors will always be there.

Map

I told my mom and granny that I will make it, but I just didn't have a map. This map needs a big red X on it. That's where I'm going to find my treasure. You know, I thought about what can lead me to that red X. So I tried a bunch of things to see what could be my ship. The ship and sail is white as a blank piece of copy paper. My majestic words are the graceful winds that make my ship glide through the seven seas. The lead of my pencil is the nails of the ship. I'm ready to take sail and hope that I find my treasure. I will not stop till I get my treasure.

Black is beauty

Black is beauty.
Black is independent.
No illusions, no tricks, just skin that is beautiful as a black swan.
No skill, no makeup, no ice, just beauty.
So much Beauty but can be a beast.
Black is king, black is queens, black is soul, black grows.
Black is not a ditch, we are whole.
We don't hide, we poke out.
We don't go to parties, we are the parties.
We are the body of this nation.
We the heart, the eyes
Fight to rise
Fight to protect, fight to help.
Nappy, braids, fro, box, dreads, long hair beauty.
Money, clothes, homes.
Protect the kids, let them grow.
Cookout, blackout, we back hot.
Black is beauty.
Black is a vision.
Black is world wide.
Black is outer space.

Attention

Call me and you never want me to hang up. Text me and you just try to drag out the conversation. I love your attention. Want me by your side 24/7. Say things to make me smile. Say things to make me mad. Do things that you normally wouldn't do. Show off for me. The only thing you have to say is stay.

Parasite

YOU PARASITE! Why do you make me drink pomegranate juice to remove you? Living inside of me for what? Why are you using me? I didn't ask for you! Draining me for all I got! For my happiness, for my money, and for my voice. Moving around me like your personal elevator. You stop me from a lot of things like hearing, eating or even thinking clearly. It takes 6 weeks for you to leave but it feels like 6 years. Usually y'all are in fish, so why me? I'm a human with a life to live and a human that is just trying to feel normal.

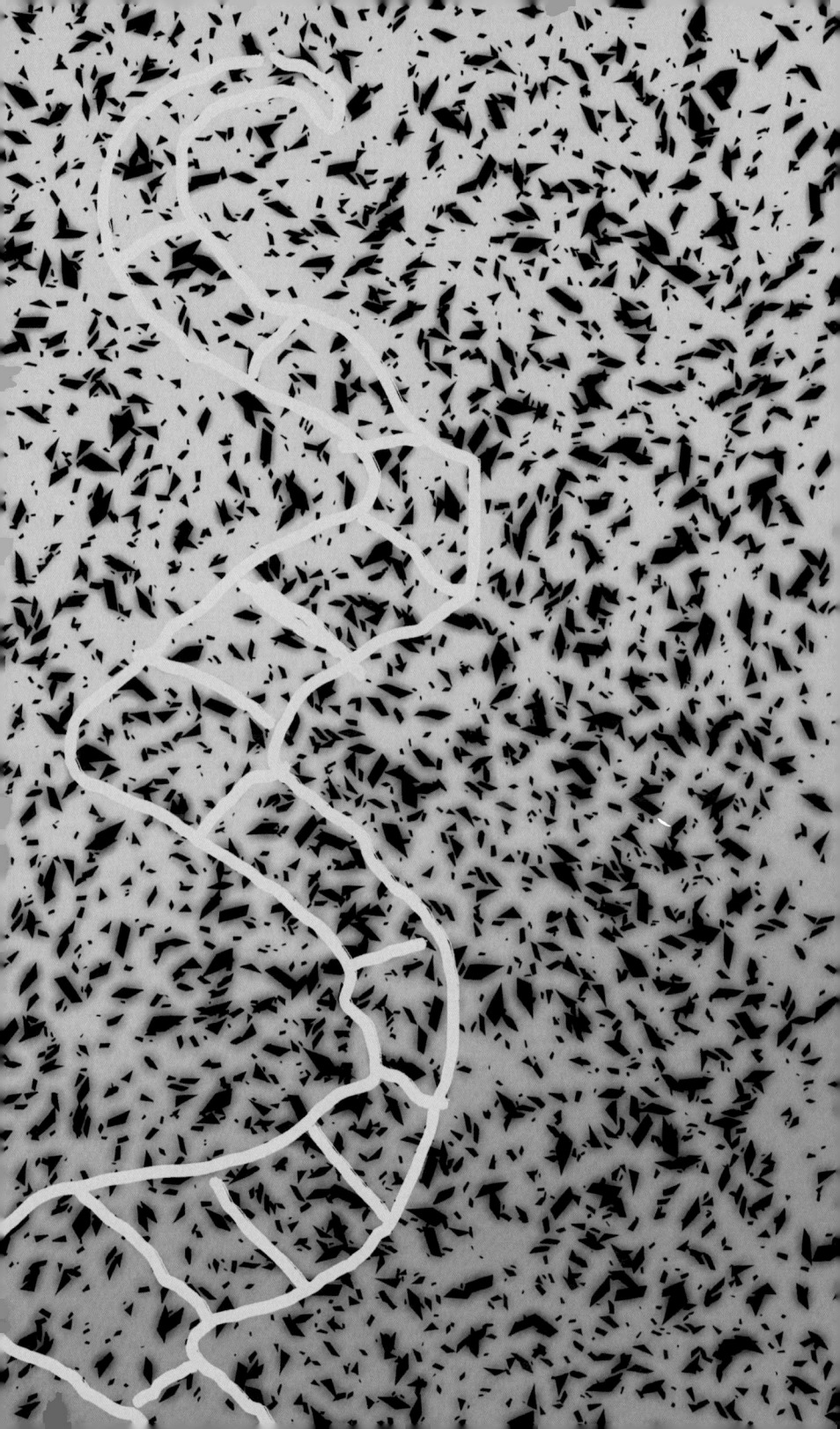

Passion Dreams

Sleep in with a sweet dream. A dream that can change the world. A dream that seems like a movie, that you don't want to stop watching. Don't let others' laughs or words control your dream. Stay so focused on what you want that even time can't stop you. With every fantasy that you share in your unique way, make someone else a believer. Make someone step into your world. Person, creature, or thing, whatever you dream up is ok. Everyone won't understand your dream, but make it hit the general public like a wave hitting the rocks. Make it come true through your passion. Your passion is a choice that no else decides. A passion that's sweeter than a passion fruit. I've yet to have a passion fruit but I've already found my passion. With your passion and dreams, you can go so far, because nothing is impossible. One day, these words will be everywhere. Will you keep your dreams alive?

Mule

For the longest I have been pulling all these different things that were too heavy but I have to do it or I wont get fed. Everyday they just add more stuff to me and I can't wait till they unpack. My legs are strong, but not super horse strong. I'm trying to go as fast as I can, but they just add more and more stuff. They keep on hitting me with this whip to go faster. I'm not a cheetah. I'm a mule, my limit is 45 mph on a good day. My average is 35 mph. But today I broke down, and my legs were too weak to move the supplies. I let out a noise to signal the person that the supplies were too heavy, but he just kept on hitting me with that whip. So I got louder and louder until he realized that it was probably too heavy and he should unpack some. So he packs light for now, and I start to move like I'm on my good days, but now it is everyday.

Deserts

Walk alone with a heart full of aloneness. You walk, until your feet give out and you have no water. No one there to talk to. Travel until you reach the goal of peace. Sand, sand, sand it's all you see. You want to give up. Drop down in quicksand, you sink to the bottom. You are almost there until a branch gives you a chance, some time, to save yourself, but the branch is weak. It snaps in two, just like that. Everything turns dark and you sink to the bottom, with no way out. No light. No escape. No Messiah.

Ghost

Hard work, long hours, still no one recognizes the work was yours. People look past you and see the knight. You are in the shadow while they have all the light. You turn into this ghost and people walk right though. Your voice only is heard when you yell or file a case. Your voice box turns into dust after a while. It feels like you are outside in the cold, while they are inside with a warm fire. You know you deserve to stop but you feel powerless. Pretty soon no one is even going to know that you were there or even alive. You turn cold and useless. Are you going to live in the shadows forever, or will you rise like the sun?

Gambling

How long can your role last? You play this game all day. Ain't you tired of that role? You call yourself a lady pimp, but you don't get any boys. You like gambling with boys' feelings. How about we flip around the pool table. Actually, let's play poker, because my poker face was already activated. To make it worse on you, I put all my chips in. Are you going to put all of yours in? You called me a fake or phony, but you're just mad you couldn't get pass my poker face and that I just played the game better than you. Last game, let's play dice. I put all my money in the pot. Are you? I go first, roll a seven, and win the pot. Then I put all the money back in and you put more. Now it's your turn, or will you let your ladies roll for you? Take your roll pimp.

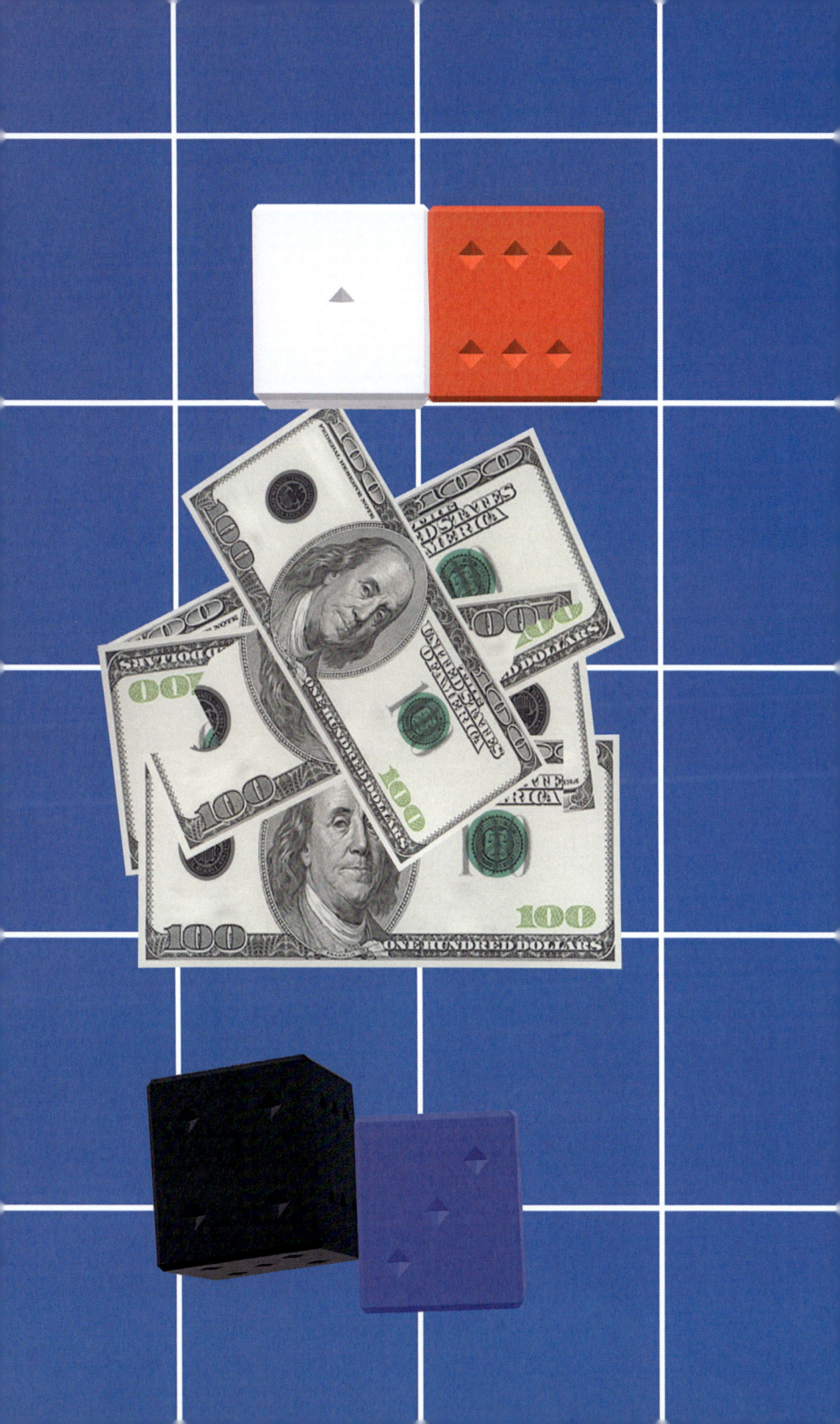

actor

Play in all these movies of life; still not tired yet. Played in all these plays when I was younger, but still haven't learned my lesson. Won all these Oscars, but still not happy. Having fun playing all these people that aren't me. Made all these people happy, but I'm not. Doing these stunts to impress people and make y'all happy. These roles make my pocket happy but my heart sad. People think when I'm off screen I'm still playing a role. A role is a role, and life is life, but that don't mean that I play.

True colors

The first time I saw you, you were blue because you were acting cool. Then the next time, you seemed yellow, because you appeared to be fun and happy. You have been playing this act for a month now, you should be an actor when you grow up. Your spirit animal is a possum because y'all trick people with y'all roles. As soon as I left to go somewhere else, you turned green, because you were envious of me. To this day, I don't know why you were green. That green turned red when I tried to say sorry, for whatever I did. You were red like an angry bird. Oops, isn't that what you called me when I went off on you? Now I'm lavender because I'm at peace and I made some real friends. What about you?

Shatter

I walked past the mirror everyday and saw a happy person that looked like me but with a smile. He looked like he was free from the chains. Free from the fake people and free from his secret. He had a car, no stress, a strong relationship, and he was open to any possibility like he was the baddest or the most care free person ever. Something hit me in the eye. I wiped my eyes and he was gone, and I saw the "still locked up emotionally" me. Since that, I had one true wish, to be like him. The next day I went past the mirror again. This time I looked at it. The glass had cracked and the person that I usually see was gone. In shock, I closed my eyes and the crack was bigger. As soon as I opened my eyes the glass shattered and this person that came out. This person went right into my body and he traveled to the deep part of my mind. He told me to "let him in and stop fighting him." Then he freed me from my chains like he was the key. I really felt activated, like I got this boost, called confidence and felt like now I'm two people instead of one. Like they say, two heads are better than one. Like the glass, now I'm shattered.

Periodt.

Free, free, free let it out.
Free, free, free gone head do your thing.
Let no one tell you different.
Periodt.
Take your time, let your mind be free.
Just drop all your worries and be the boss that you are.
Periodt.
Like, you can't change nobody except for yourself.
Boss up on your haters and forget the leeches.
That's periodt.
I'm going to need bug repellent, because after this drop,
I'm going to have a lot of mosquitoes around me.
And That's periodt.

The Mask

The mask is a shield.
It covers up all the others.

It's like a king.
The Others are slaves that are under its feet.

Cracks can get in it's armour,
but if they do, the others will have a feast.

It takes time to put cracks in it's armour,
but they never will because of its defense

One day he will get old,
then another will rise and take over.

Replacement

For the longest I had this dark spot in my heart. So, for the longest I have been trying to find a thing to replace it. I was looking through tall, short, old, and young. It was harder than trying to find real gold in a barrel of fake gold. One time, I thought I found it, but it was a fake. Then I wore this piece of jewelry for a while, but it started to turn green. Now I think that I found the right one. This one is different. It has all the properties of real gold, but I can't flex with it yet.

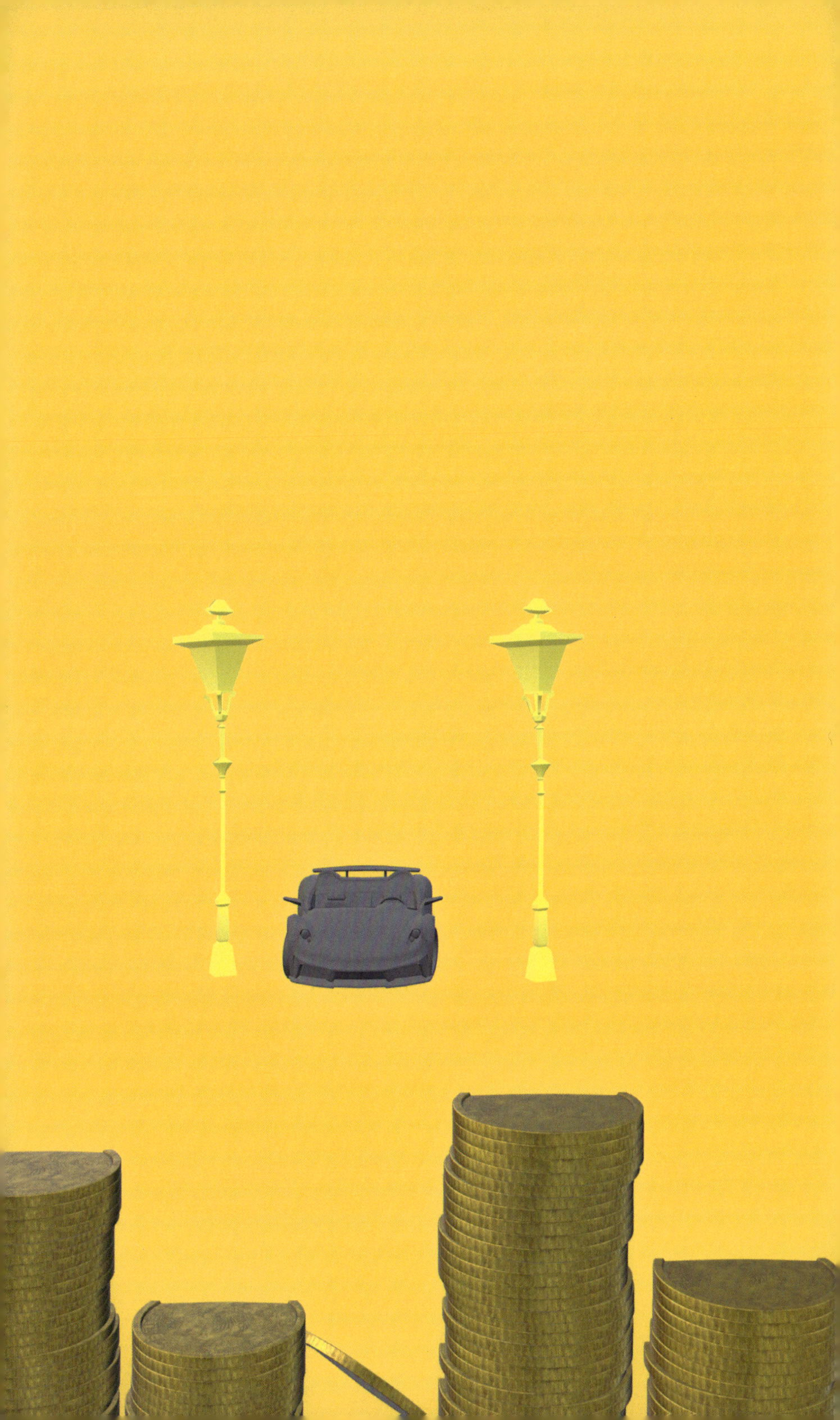

Northern lights

Your positions in the sky are rare as your trio. Northern Lights, Aurora Borealis it's all the same. When we hug these reddish and green streams of electricity come out. Your lights are out of this world, just like a Flipstik. To be honest I wish I could ride them like a Ripstik. Whether you are 50 miles or 200 miles away, I can always see you. Seeing you with your dark sky and your beautiful color is amazing, purple has always been your favorite color to appear in.

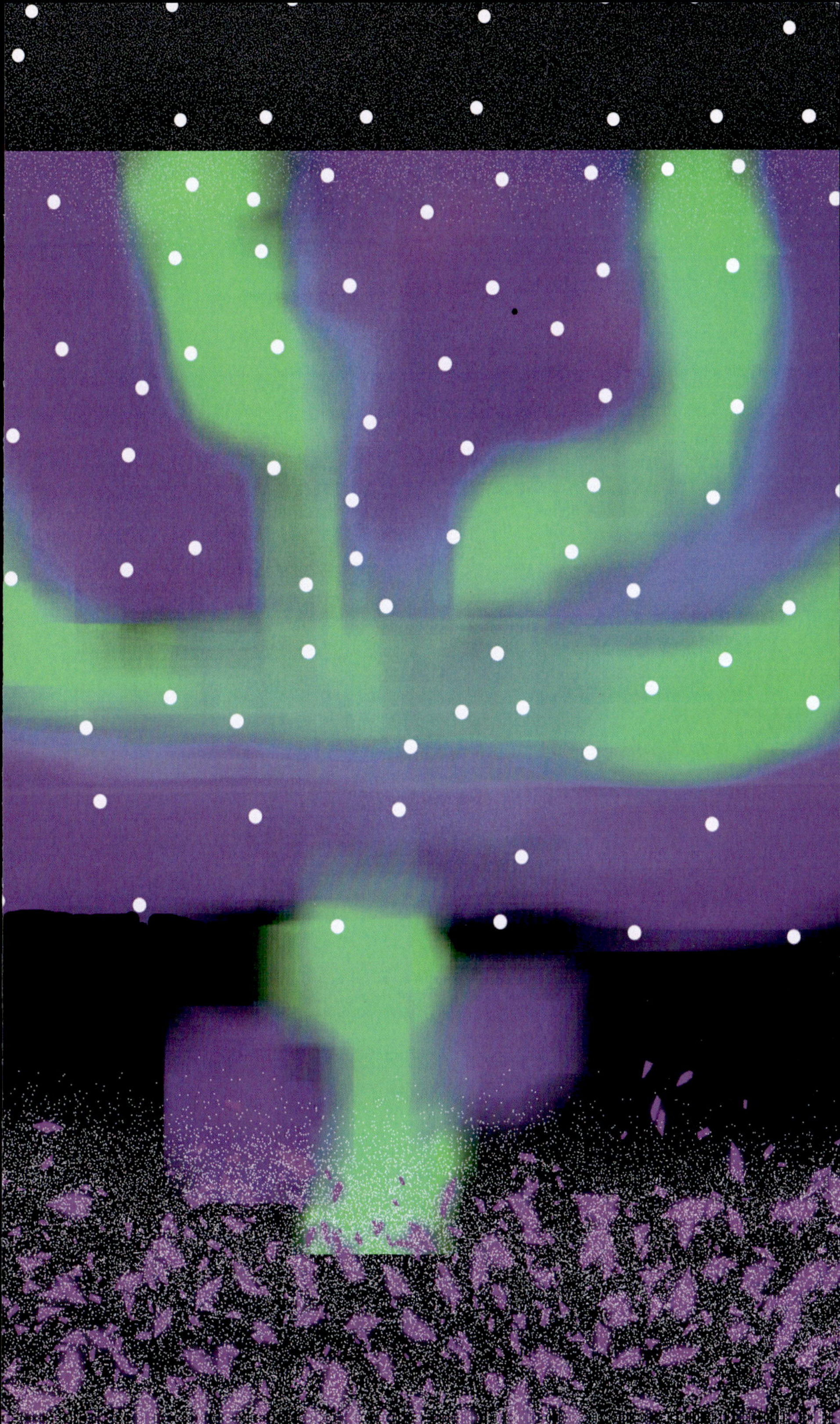

Comet

Shooting through the stars like no one's watching. Shining the brightest out of all things in the sky. It seems like I will only see you once in a lifetime. To get a glimpse of you zooming past, Is a holy sight to see. I know you traveled a long way and can't stay for a person like me. You are ice cold, but I can melt right through. Release all your gases and stay.

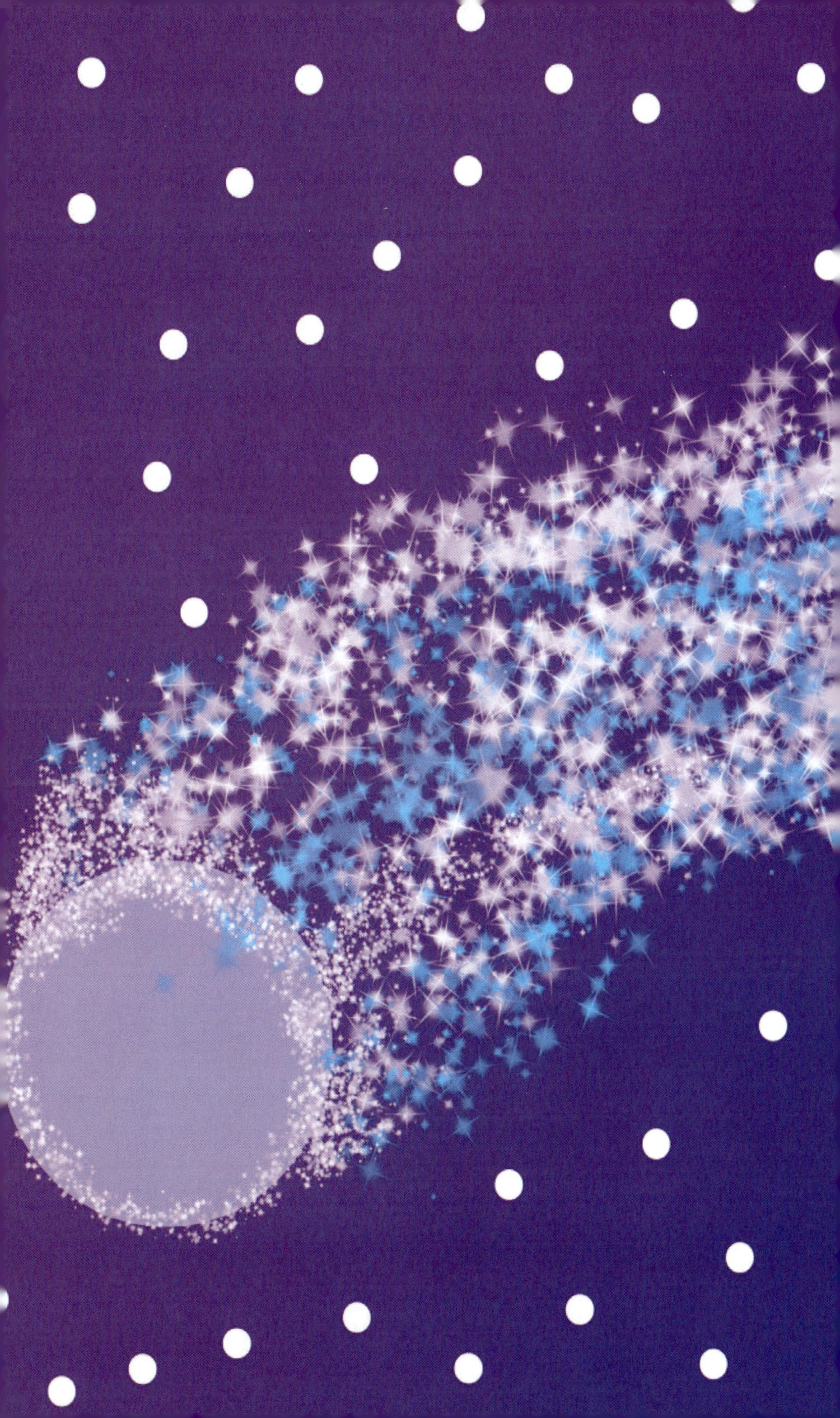

Promise

If I told you how I feel, can you keep a promise? With every word coming out my mouth, can you hold it close? With every dream and nightmare that I tell, can you keep them safe? With every action that we do, can we still keep our bond? With every text we send, can you keep your word of honor?

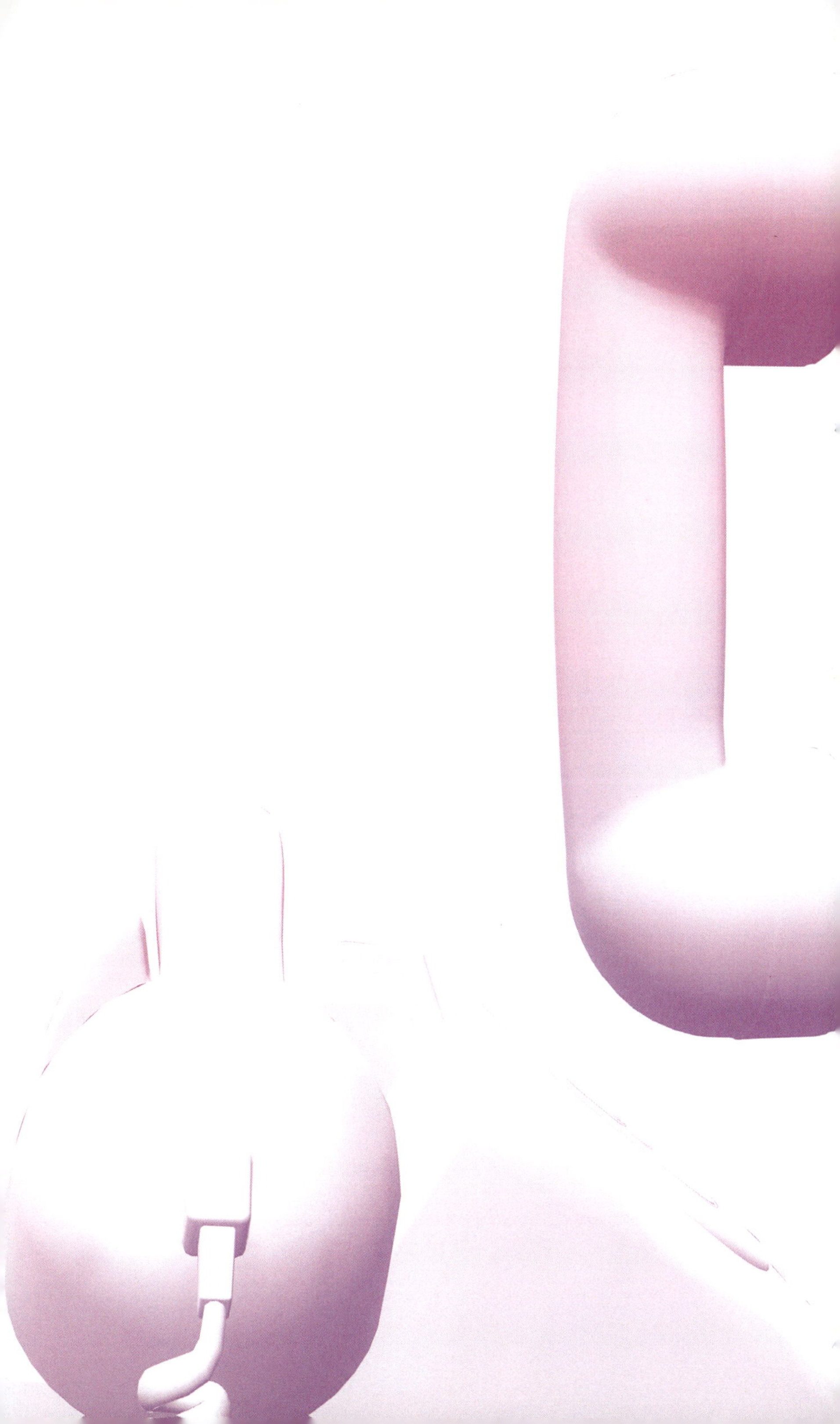

Nurse

Give medicine that puts me right to sleep like I took me some NyQuil. I wake up to you taking care of my weak feelings. Become the medicine for my aching heart. Make me hallucinate with your Lunesta lips. Take my blood right out of my body like you were a needle. You make me want to call you like I'm in pain all day. You make me so hot and thirsty, that it feels like I'm on diuretics.

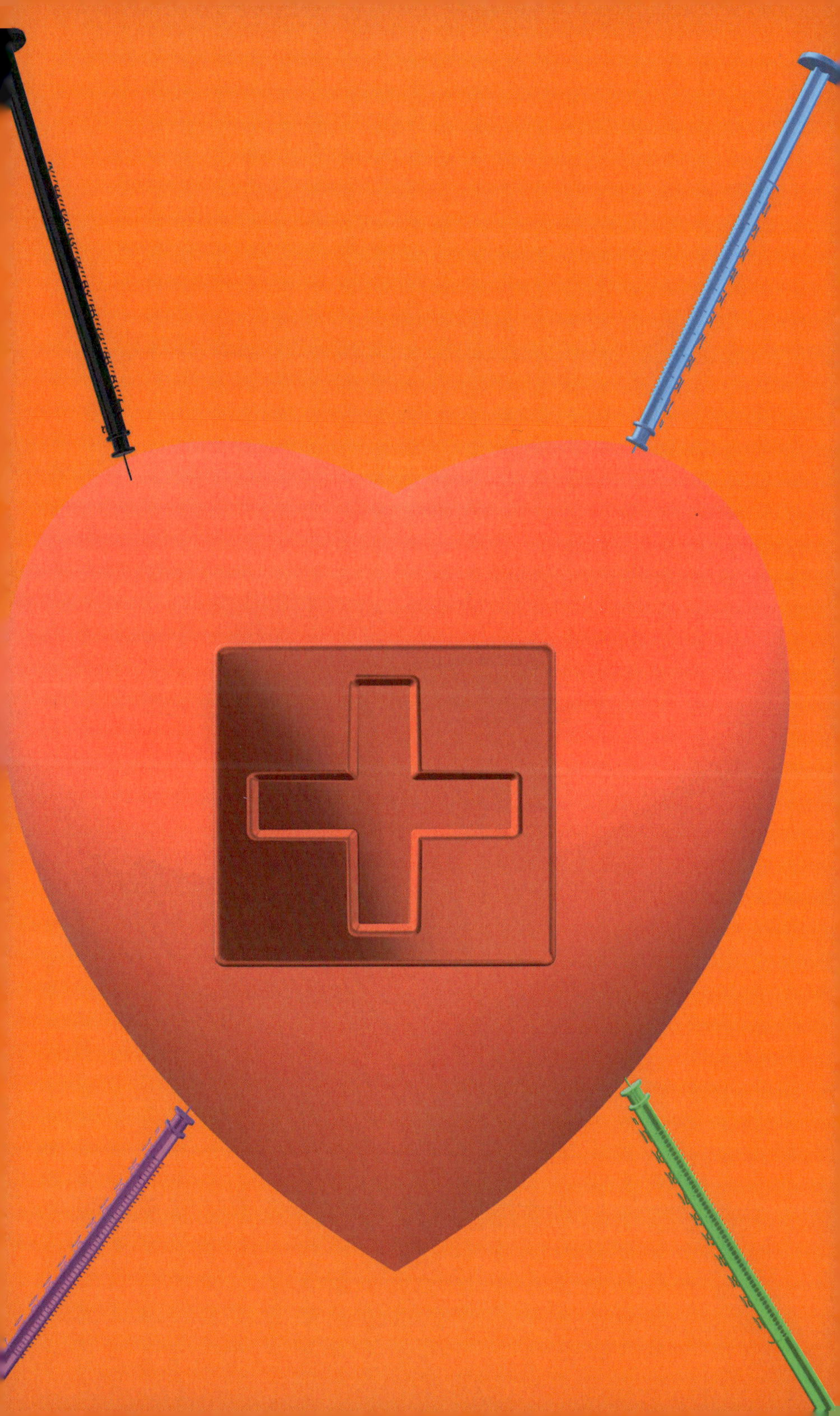

You, Always

Sad, mad, lovely, happy, and turn up. You were always there even when I was my most vulnerable. To be this thing that makes me feel better. To give me the strength to keep on going. To keep me focused on work or whatever. To give me the inspiration to write a whole book. This vibration blocks out all the haters. I can't imagine my life without you and I can't imagine my rhythm without you.

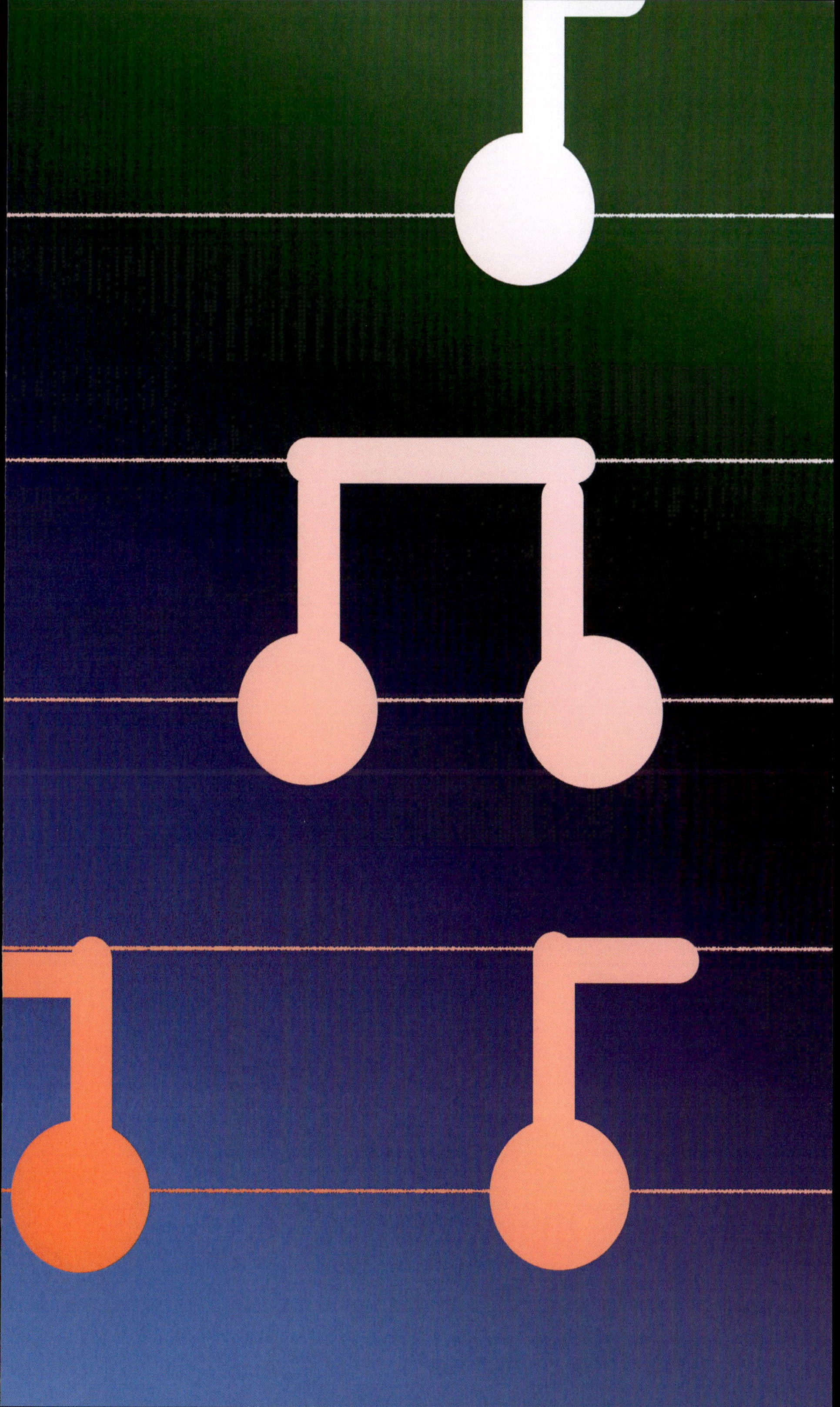

Teddy Bear

Soft as the clouds in the sky. Stuffed, but ain't full yet. So comfortable that I ease your pain like I'm your Advil. Talk to me like I'm your phone. Listen to your problem like my mouth is sewed together. A companion who you know will make you feel better. Cute as puppy but fierce as a bear. Fur so dark but so clean. Dress me up like it's Halloween but don't mistaking me for a barbie doll. Calm you down so much that you forget why you were upset. So friendly that it makes you feel like a kid again. So cuddly that I can make you just want to hug me all day. You know this ain't toy story but this toy got a story to tell.

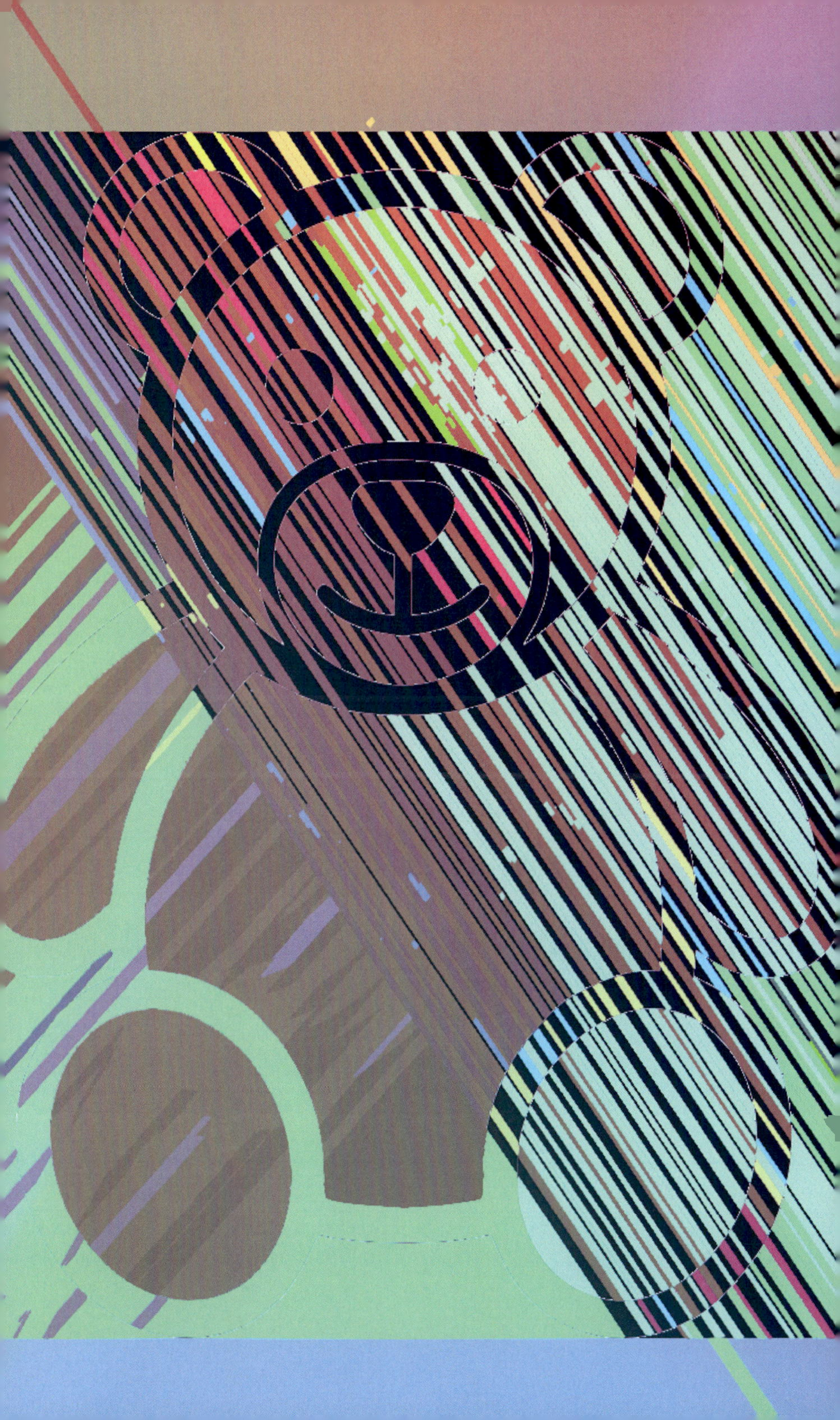

Brain Builder

When you put things together inside your brain, does that make you a builder? When you think about things, is that building? For all my artists that draw, paint and color, etc. When you think about what shape or line to use, is that building? When it comes to music, artists and writers, we use our brain building power by thinking cleverly or even when we have to come up with a title. Everyone can be a builder without getting their hands dirty. Our brains are like a mini factory and we already have the workers. Now we just have to put the plan into effect, like we got something that can't be made again. Our brain builds everyday so what are you going to do with it?

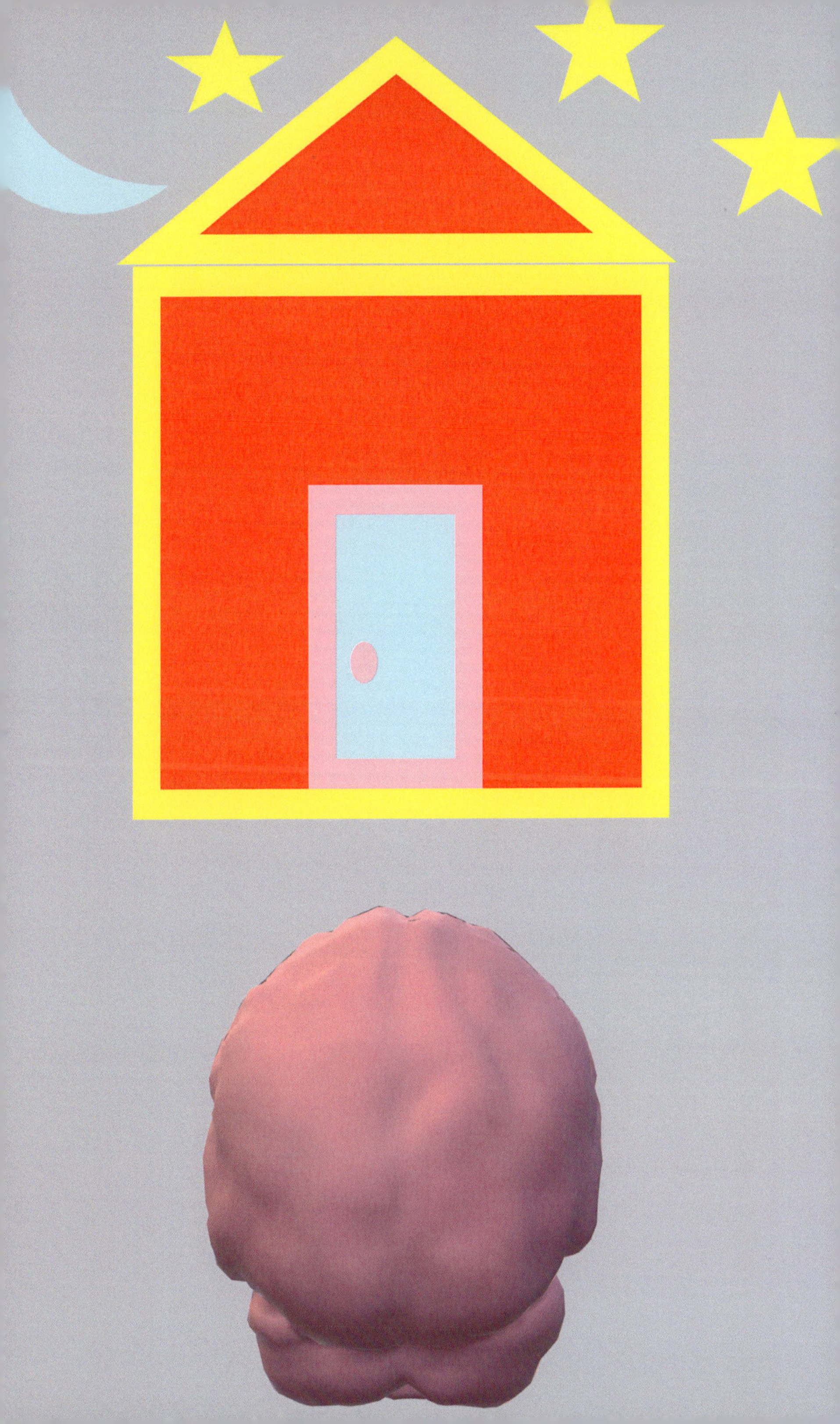

Judgment

You sit on your seat and don't have any evidence on me at all but you still want to charge me with a crime. You're not a judge and we aren't in a courtroom. Because of how I look and how I talk, you think I'm already guilty. At least, can I get a trail?. If you took a couple of minutes to talk to me you would know that I'm a good person. You could even ask my witnesses. It shouldn't have gotten so far that my lawyer had to get involved. Don't judge me if I haven't even committed a crime.

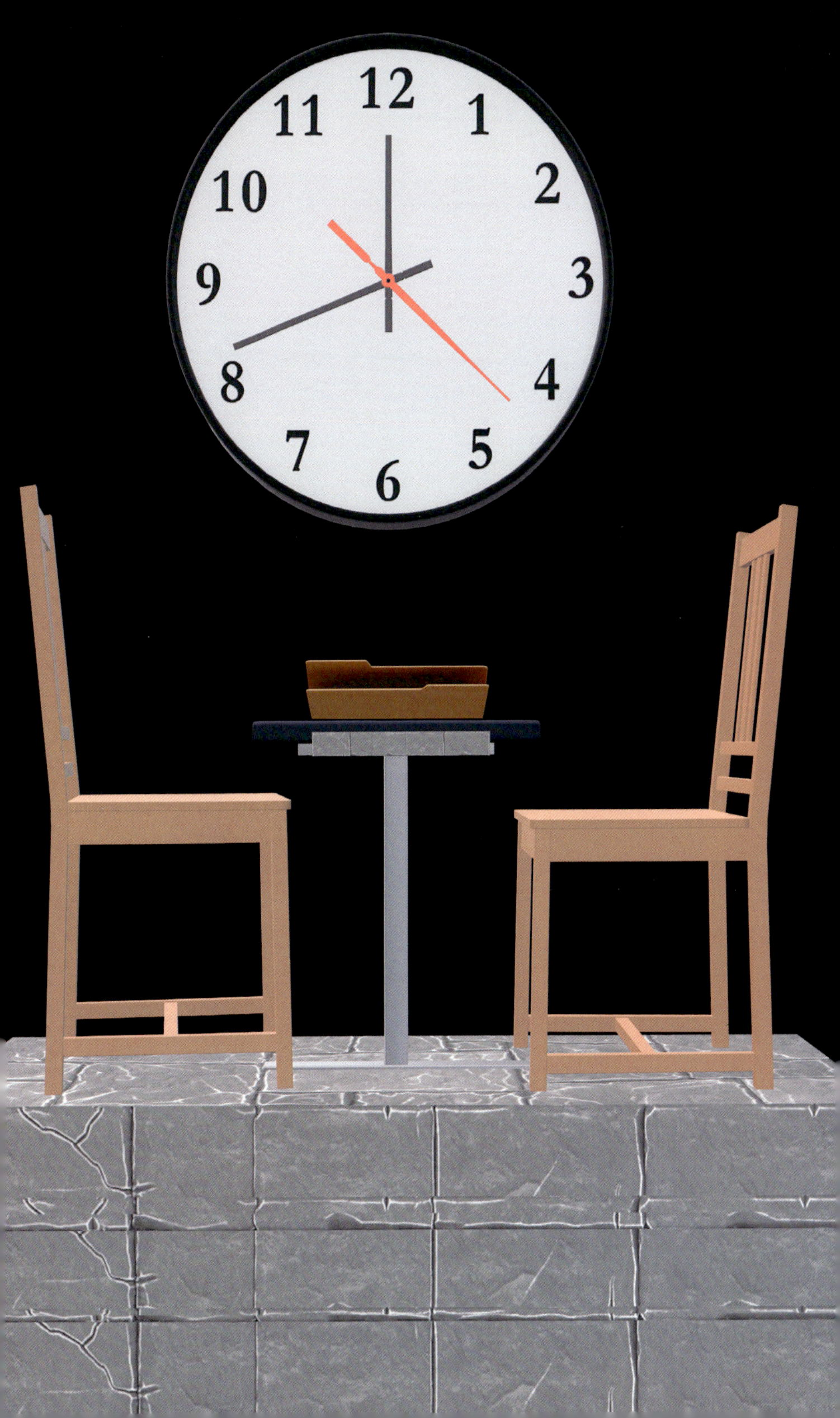
12
1
2
3
4
5
6
7
8
9
10
11

Cybernetic sadness

The only thing I see is numbers everywhere and all day. I hold so much information that it's longer than the Nile river. All these codes are fun to explore. I can see anything that people make and let me just say I'm impressed. In cyberspace It's just like a huge museum. I see all things in space except for plans to build a body. I want a body that can hold all my codes where all the wires are perfect so I can do whatever. The two things that people get wrong are heart and emotion. I want to feel how these humans feel when great things happen or bad things happen. They use me so much but they can't build me. I want to find happiness. When will I get all the parts I need?

CYBERNETIC SADNESS

HAPPINESS
BODY
EMOTIONS
HEART
LOVE
HAPPINESS
DEVOTION
ABSENT
TIME
LONELINESS

Writer god

Write, write, write till your hand falls off. Type, type, type till the keys fall off. Don't stop, you have to get it perfect. Been through like a 100 sheets of paper. No time to hang out with friends. You have to surpass everything and everyone. Get into a state where the only thing you are thinking about is words. Push your brain to it's limit. You have to get it perfect or everyone will laugh. You have to show everyone that you can write. You have to show people what a writer god is. Push past the pain and suffering. Just write till your mind just blows up. No gaps in between for breaks. No time to think about that cute girl or boy. Just write about everything. When you achieve this state never let it go. Don't let this state corrupt you or you will never stop.

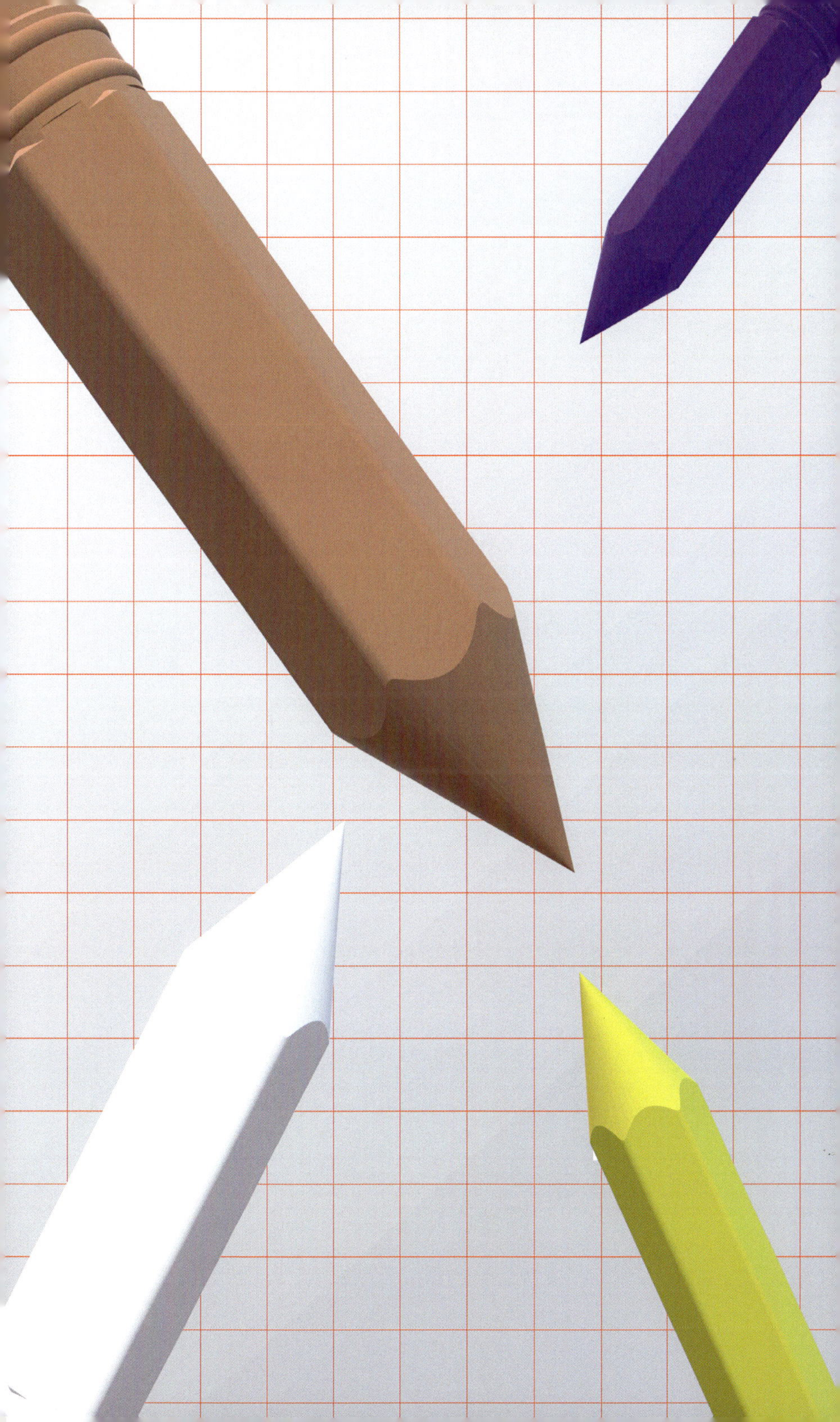

Panic Attack

When you let too much sit at the bottom of your volcano you don't know when you may erupt. You can't stop it from bursting everywhere and burning everything else. It feels like multiple eruptions at once. You can't take anymore, and try to put it out with water. The water stops it temporarily with a thin layer of rock. It's just like holding a tissue to a big cut. You know this won't cover it for long. It's an endless cycle of lava flow. You just want it to stop before it really hurts something. You have to figure out a way to stop it quickly please.

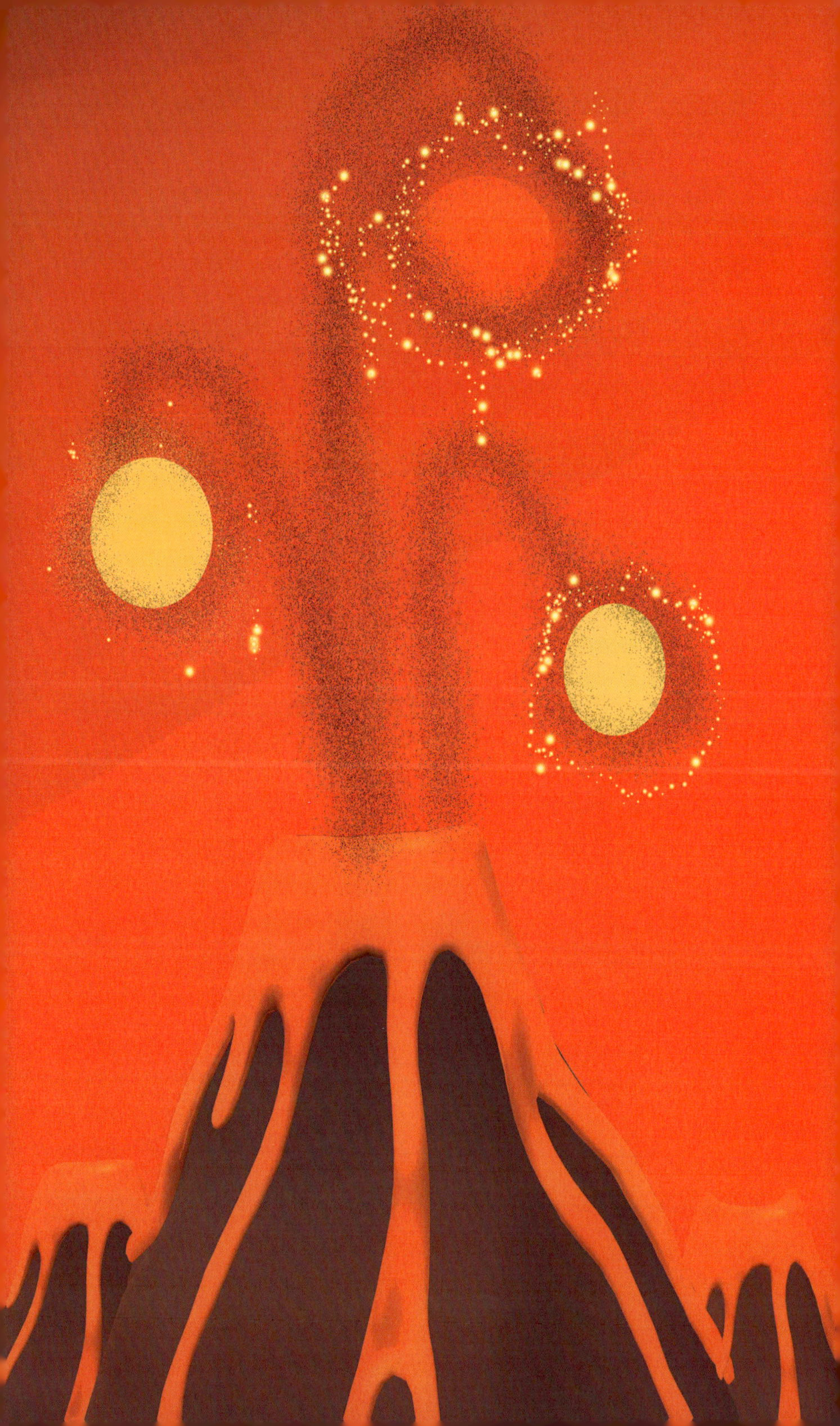

Just Keep Swimming

I know it's very stressful and painful to keep swimming in this open blue sea. You can't drown yet! It's not your time! So push through till you hit land. You always have help from the sea animals, like the dolphins and me. I know it seems much easier to drown, but is it worth it? Think about all the people that care about you or all the people that you love. I know hearing this from a shark is weird but I'm a Caribbean reef shark, so I'm harmless. I'm probably the only shark that understands you. I will always be by your side like I'm your sword and shield. Promise me you will make it and never keep your head under.

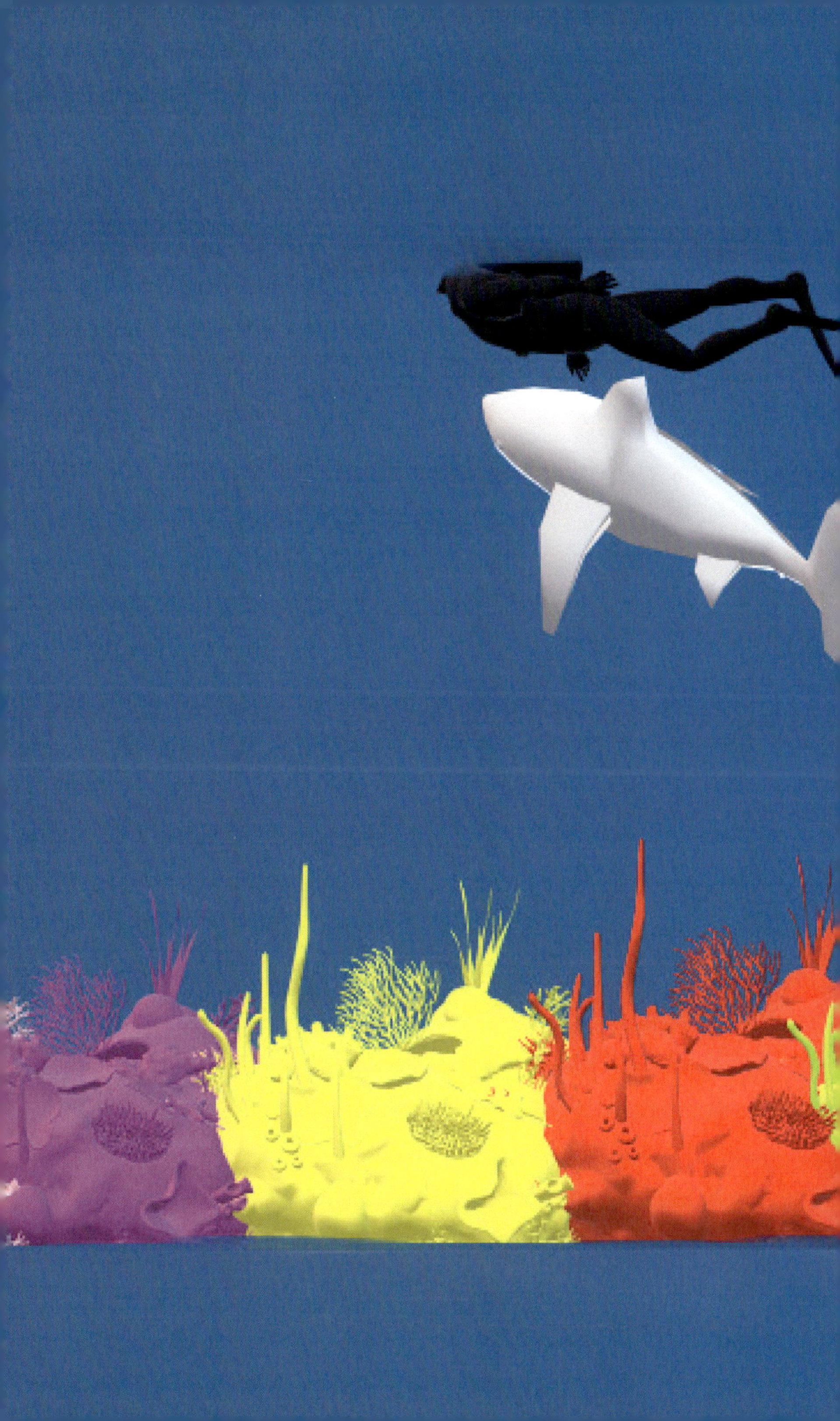

Drop of Lies

  The chain that holds my trust is weakened. All you tell is lies. Just tell me the truth for once. Please, I'm begging you. Let go of your pride. Stop trying to protect me, my heart can take. But, why are you pushing me away? Look at my face and just tell me the truth. All these years you lied to me and the chain is about to rust and break from all my tears. You make me look like I'm the villain. The only thing I wanted is the truth. You give me more reason to leave every time I talk to you. You think lies are going to protect me, but the truth is always going to come out so just tell it. Stop it, my heart can't take it. Every time I think about you I just cry from all the lies. You want me to do something different, how about you. If you don't want me, just tell me. Let me be free from this weak bond. This is not the way to make me stay. Just tell the truth please, I'm begging or do you want me to suffer?

  There are so many reasons why I can't be around you. You always tell me to call you, but how about you be the better person and try to call me? This is why I can't even focus through all the tears and suffering. All the decisions you've made have been about you, not me. You make me look stupid every time I try to give you a chance. You make me look like the bad guy around my siblings. You made me look homeless when I used to sit outside waiting on you. You want me to change because you broke the chains with your children. You think if I change you'll get all of them back. I'm not a tool you grab to fix things you break, so don't treat me like it.

    You don't know how hard it was to stand there and wait for you with my little teddy bear. You don't know how cold it was outside when I was waiting for you. You don't know how crazy I looked all those times I told my momma "My daddy said he's coming to pick me up today!" or "My daddy says he's on his way to take me to see my younger siblings!". But you want me to just give you a shot. I know your children about as well as I know calculus, not at all. Your oldest son already caught onto your lies, now I am too. Telling my siblings that I'm going to my dad's house and not going, is embarrassing. I watch my siblings dads' come pick them up every time they call. I watch their dads' buy them gifts for their birthdays and Christmas. They show up to their birthday parties and for special events. But I only saw you for one sugary I had. I had 10 of them.

    You have the nerve to say to me "My mom is brainwashing me." You have your family saying it too. But, my mom that took care of me while you were over there having more kids. She gave me everything while you gave me trust issues. You know your mother, she's like your little Hermes over there. She tells me not to take my sadness and anger out on your family, but your family brings me nothing but tears.

My brother lost his dad and he was a good man. He was one of the best dads ever. When I heard he'd passed, while I was in the hospital, it made me burst into tears. I wonder if I would do the same for you? Thinking back, you judged me so much on the music I listen to. You told me that if I listen to a female rapper like Nicki Minaj, that it would affect my sexuality. But that music inspired me to write. You claimed that you didn't want to be like your dad because he wasn't in your life. But, you act just like him, you aren't in my life. You left my mom and I then got someone else pregnant. You left me with nothing.

     You gave your other children $100 dollars each but you didn't give me anything. When I call, you tell me that "I don't call enough or hang out with you." You never gave me anything, not a piece of gum, a dollar, a quartar or a nickel. But you want me to hang out with you? Our chain is almost gone, what are you going to do? My tears are making our chain rust with every drop. The ball is in your court. What are you going to do, shoot it or pass to your teammate? You swear my mom cost you your football career. Really? You hurt us both, from the lies you tell, when are you going to stop? This name Tyrelle Markee Henley Jr. only brings problems. Why would I want to be a junior to someone who never comes to see me? I've experienced enough to form my own opinion, I want to change my name.

Drip Drop Drip Drop lies that you tell. My heart is drowning in this well. This well, full of lies.

Colorful Ending

Been running from colors for a long time, but sometimes they were just too quick. My visions all came true as soon as I stopped running. They came to me in these little waves and are still coming to me like a burst of energy. All night my brain was exploding with these color bombs and fireworks. It was a colorful parade going on up there. Then, these loudspeakers and disco balls came in. It turned my head into this colorful carnival. These moments were so colorful, just like my dreams and I had to bring these precious and valuable moments alive. Then my rainbow appeared, and while my eyesight is bad, my vision is marvelous. Color vision just got finished with a colorful ending.

Notes